BRIEFLY SINGING

ROBIN SKELTON

SELECTED AND IN ENGLISH VERSIONS

Sono Nis Press
VICTORIA, B.C., CANADA

BRIEFLY
SINGING

A GATHERING OF EROTIC
SATIRICAL
AND OTHER
INSCRIPTIONS EPIGRAMS
AND LYRICS
FROM THE GREEK AND ROMAN
MEDITERRANEAN

800 BC – AD 1000

INCLUDING THE COMPLETE POEMS
OF RUFINUS

Copyright © 1994 by Robin Skelton

Canadian Cataloguing in Publication Data

Skelton, Robin, 1925-
   Briefly singing

   Poems.
   ISBN 1-55039-048-1

   I. Title
PS8537.K38B7 1994   C811'.54   C94-910233-4
PR9199.3.S53B7 1994

Published with assistance of the
Canada Council Block Grant Program.

Published by
SONO NIS PRESS
1745 Blanshard Street
Victoria, British Columbia V8W 2J8

Designed and printed in Canada by
MORRISS PRINTING COMPANY LTD.
Victoria, British Columbia

*To
the memory of*
BONAMY DOBREE
*my mentor and friend,
who introduced me
to Rufinus.*

CONTENTS

11 Introduction

I THE CLASSICAL PERIOD

19 Alkman
20 Anakreon
23 Appollodoros
24 Archilochus
26 Demodocus
27 Epicharmus
28 Hegemon of Alexandria
29 Hipponax
30 Ibykos
31 Mimnermos
32 Perses
33 Phokylides
34 Plato
36 Praxilla
37 Sappho
42 Semonides of Amorgos
43 Simonides of Ceos
44 Socrates
45 Solon
46 Stesichoros
47 Theognis
48 Timocreon
49 Thucydides the Historian
50 Tymnes
51 Xenophanes

II THE ALEXANDRIAN PERIOD

- 55 Alkaios
- 57 Anyte
- 58 Antipater of Sidon
- 59 Ariston
- 60 Asclepiades
- 62 Asklepiades
- 65 Antipater of Thessalonica
- 66 Calimachus
- 68 Crates
- 69 Crinagoras
- 70 Dionysius of Andros
- 71 Dionysius of Herclea
- 72 Dionysius of Sophist
- 73 Dioscorides
- 75 Diotimos
- 76 Hedylus
- 77 Leonidas of Tarentum
- 79 Meleager
- 85 Mnasalkes
- 86 Nossis
- 87 Phalaikos
- 88 Philip V of Macedon
- 89 Philitas
- 90 Posidippus
- 91 Theodoridas
- 92 Theokritos
- 93 Zenodotos

III THE ROMAN PERIOD

- 97 Addaeus of Macedon
- 98 Antipator
- 99 Antipater of Thessalonica
- 101 Antiphanes
- 102 Archias
- 104 Automedon

105	Bassus
106	Bianor
108	Erycius
109	Evenus of Ascalon
110	Gaetulicus
111	Honestus
112	Isidorus Scholasticus
113	Maecius
114	Marcus Argentarius
117	Myrinus
118	Parmenion
119	Philodemus
122	Pinytos
123	Statyllius Flaccus
124	Diodorus Zonas

IV AND FROM THE LATIN

127	Pacuvius
128	Sulpicia
129	Horace
131	Hadrian
132	Petronius
133	Catullus
136	Martial

V THE PERIOD OF THE EMPIRE

145	Ammianus
146	Ammonides
147	Antiphilus of Byzantium
149	Appollinarius
150	Cillactor
151	Callicter
152	Capito
153	Claudianus
154	Cyrillus
155	Democritus
156	Diogenes Laertius

157 Diophanes of Myrina
158 Evodus
159 Fronto
160 Geminus
161 Glaucus
162 Glycon
163 Saint Gregory the Theologian
164 Irenaeus Referendarius
165 Julian the Apostate
166 Leonidas of Alexandria
167 Lucian
169 Lucilius
172 Metrodorus
174 Nicarchus
175 Philemon
176 Palladas
181 Phillipus
182 Philippus of Thessalonika
184 Rufinus
200 Satyrus
201 Strato
207 The Emperor Trajan

VI THE BYZANTINE PERIOD

211 Agathias
212 Damaskios
213 Erotosthenes Scholasticus
214 Julian Antecessor
215 Julianus, Prefect of Egypt
217 Macedonius the Consul
218 Paul the Silentiary
225 Plato the Younger
226 Constantine Cephalas

VII ANONYMOUS

229 Anonymous

INTRODUCTION

Twenty years have elapsed since I published my collection of *Two Hundred Poems from the Greek Anthology* and the book has been long out of print. Although it was well received in general I now find it inadequate as an overview of the epigrams, inscriptions and lyrics of Ancient Greek and the Roman and Byzantine Empires. For one thing the anthology, even in its most comprehensive edition, omits Anakreon and other poets of the period before 350 BC and Anakreon and the Anakreontea of his followers provided much of the foundation upon which the later poetry was based. Sappho, moreover, that extraordinary poet so frequently praised by poets of later centuries, is also not included. Surveying the period again I also realized that at least two Latin poets should be included – Catullus because he was, in Peter Jay's words, "the greatest epigrammatist of the period between Meleager and Philip" (roughly 100 BC–AD 50). Moreover his lyrics are similar in many respects to those of the Alexandrian Greek poets he admired. Martial, I felt, also belonged to the company. He lived from around AD 40 to AD 104, at a time when the Greek Epigrammatists and lyrists were in full flower, and, indeed, we are told that he had some influence upon his Greek contemporaries as upon later poets. He, himself, had clearly learned from the Greek tradition, and it was initially by way of Martial that the poets of the English Renaissance, especially Ben Jonson, came to understand the use of classical brevities. Considering both Catullus and Martial led me to look at Horace once again and to feel that he, too, demanded a little space, and I chose two poems that repeat standard themes of his Greek contemporaries and forebears. Pacuvius' epitaph on himself I simply could not bear to leave out.

In making these English Versions I have emulated other translators in taking certain liberties with the originals, interpreting and qualifying them, substituting current images for ancient ones, and sometimes providing an English equivalent for a pun or quip that, if literally translated, would fall flat or be incomprehensible. In my earlier collection I said that, as a translator, I had adopted what might be called a "double standard" and went on to say:

> In the case of those poems which are informal in tone and uncluttered with allusions, I have deliberately modernized both the names and the diction. These, in fact, might more properly be called "versions" than translations, for I have not tried to keep too close to the letter of the originals, preferring to make new poems which have as many of the qualities of the old as possible, but which do not necessarily carry precisely the same shades of meaning. Exact translation is often an enemy to the provision of an artistic equivalent. When we read a delightful little love-poem addressed to a girl by a young man in a fit of affection and exuberance, the whole spontaneity is lost if the name of the girl is given as Rhodope. The poem becomes immediately a piece of antiquity instead of a part of our own existence. Consequently, in making these versions I have done my best to use only English proper names. Of course, some proper names have had to remain in the Greek. I could hardly translate *Zeus* as *God* without making a fool of myself, and there are some witty references to Greek myth which I couldn't bear to leave out. On the whole, however, my attempt has been to place these poems in the context of our world, and to make them speak in our accents. This has meant the alteration of much imagery. In one poem I refer to "lipstick and eye-shadow" which are, obviously, un-Greek, though the Greeks did use cosmetics and the poem is about that use. In another poem high-heel shoes are substituted

for Greek sandals. In yet another I make the Greek Rose-seller an English Chocolate-and-Cigarettes girl; this helped me to imitate the play upon words of the original poem more accurately. We do, nowadays, call girls "my sweet," but we no longer refer to them, at least ordinarily, as "roses." The same wish to imitate the gesture of the original led me in other poems to exchange for the Greek wine the British ale, and to replace Hesiod's *Works and Days* with Gibbon's *Decline and Fall*, this last alteration being intended to give the reader a meaningful book-title rather than an esoteric reference, as well as to help me to a play upon words similar to that in the original.

Many poems, however, would suffer too great a transformation if modernized in this fashion. In translating the dedicatory poems, some of the sepulchral poems, and some of the more formal verses, I have therefore sometimes retained the original Greek names, and have allowed myself occasional inversions and a slightly mannered syntax which I felt would "distance" the poems to the right extent. Thus, in Archias' poem upon Apelles' statue of Cyprus I use the word "thus" which would be inappropriate in a less deliberately graceful compliment, and in Philippus of Thessalonica's dedicatory poem, while modernizing the fisherman's name to Jack, I allowed myself a plethora of picturesque epithets.

In being thus inconsistent I have, I hope, been consistent to one of my intentions, which was to display the variety of the Greek Anthology without ever departing too far from a particular norm. With the exception of the poems in Book Thirteen all the poems are in dactylic elegaic couplets. My own versions are metrically more free, but are all, for the most part, rhymed or near rhymed, and basically iambic or trochaic. The number of feet in each line may vary, but, if I am allowed to count the shorter-lined versions as being composed in half-lines, the average works out a tetrameter or pentameter. Iambic and trochaic tetrameter and pentameter are, clearly, the forms central to the English lyric tradition, and most of the previous translators of the epigrams have used rhymed quatrains in these metres. Mine is, therefore, a very conservative approach, as regards form. The forms I have used owe less to my conservatism (which is, I think, rather doubtful) than to my conviction that if one is to translate a poem from one language to another, one should think in terms of providing an equivalent form, not an imitated one. Most English poets when tackling the kind of subject that is dealt with in these poems have used neatly rhyming short-lined verse. The epigram in English is most frequently presented in the shape of a precisely rhymed quatrain, and the liveliest vernacular is most usually balanced by a strict verse form. In saying this I am, perhaps, thinking back to Ben Jonson, to the Cavaliers, to Prior, or to Landor, rather than thinking of numbers of our modern translators.

A reviewer in the *Times Literary Supplement*, who was clearly and properly a Classical scholar, took issue with me on this matter. He or she said, "the names and props of an Anthology poem were often meant to be formal, or in some subtle contrast to an expected formality; it was a matter of exact usage and resonance, a different kind of poetry from anything in English . . . the exact rhymes and clear, sharp rhythms of Gravesian English verses knock the humour and the pathos flat: the elegaic couplet was not built to withstand accentual climax, and the climax that the rhythm of English verse imposes on a short epigram is the bump of a hammer where the poem was conceived as the dying notes of a guitar."

This may be true, but the process of translation is one of "making over" from one language into another. No English translation of Dante has the cadence and flow of the Italian, and the most effective translations are those which turn the aliens of one language into the citizens of another. A more serious criticism of my approach was made by Peter Jay in his brilliantly edited collection, *The Greek Anthology*, which contained versions by many hands, including my own. Referring to my modernization of names he states that I seem "to assume that the reader has no imaginative historical sense at all" and adds that "translation puts a barrier between the reader and the idea of an authentic original which he must derive from the version, if an ancient poet called, say, Meleager, appears to be addressing amorous verses to Gloria and Janet, not to mention Gerald and Julian – with the improbable connotations such names evoke."

Peter Jay has, I think, a valid point, but it is only applicable to some of my versions, and to a smaller proportion of the whole than in my earlier collection. In these cases I have felt the raciness of the original would be obstructed for the general reader by the intrusion of strange names with dubious pronunciations. Moreover, one of the reasons for producing these versions is to show that these ancient writers can be seen, from time to time, as very much of our own world. Indeed, as I look through this collection, I see that the poems vary considerably in this regard, sometimes clearly belonging to an ancient culture, and sometimes belonging to our own, providing, I trust, pleasure for both those with an "imaginative historical sense" and those without it.

In another part of his Introduction, Peter Jay states that he had hoped originally, "to represent the work of each Greek Poet in translations by the same hand, to give some impression of a consistent original oeuvre and of a consistent approach in translation." This he found impossible, and the success of his anthology is partly due to the extraordinary variety of styles and approaches that it contains. Nevertheless, it is hard to see the Strato of Thomas Mayer as the same person as the Strato of Teddy Hogge, and the voice of Kenneth Rexroth's Asklepiades is not that of Alan Marshfield's. Much is gained by these differences; one realizes just how various translations may be, and how many-sided are the originals. On the other hand there is, perhaps, something to be gained by an over-all consistency provided by a single translator; comparisons become easier to make; similarities are more clearly perceived; and the coherence and unity of the tradition is emphasized.

In making my selections I have tried to represent all the main concerns and interests of the poets, and have, quite deliberately, included poems which echo one another. A neatly turned truism by Xenophon of the Classical Period is echoed by Palladas in the fifth century AD. A joke of Lucilius in the first century AD is repeated by Ammianus in the second. The themes that run through the whole tradition are easy to catalogue: poems of dedication, epitaphs, erotic verse, both heterosexual and homosexual, satirical comments on human frailty and reflections on mortality. Together, they add up to a portrait of humankind that is frequently amusing, often poignant, and always shrewd.

In arranging these verses I have followed convention in separating the writers into the five periods – the Classical (or Greek) Period, 700 BC–350 BC, the Hellenistic (or Alexandrian) Period, 350 BC–90 BC, the Roman Period, 90 BC–AD 50. The period of the Roman Empire AD 50–AD 450, and the Byzantine Period, AD 500 and after, I have chosen to lump all the anonymous poems together, as many of them are difficult to date. One can only say that those included in the Wreath of Meleager must have been written before the first century BC, that those in the Wreath of Philippus before the reign of Nero or Caligula, and those in the Cycle of Agathias before, or during, the reign of Justinian II, and so forth. In other words, we only know that some of them could not have been written later than a certain date, but we do not know how long they had been in circulation before they were collected. Some, of course, provide clues to their date of composition by their contents, but these are relatively few. It is likely that the anonymous poems, as a group, range over the whole period, and they do, indeed, provide a kind of overview, if they are all placed together.

I

THE
CLASSICAL
PERIOD

700 BC – AD 350

ALKMAN (7TH CENTURY BC)

Life's pathway is both steep and narrow
and need knows neither shame nor sorrow.

ANAKREON (563–478 BC)

1

In a cheap shiny suit
frayed grey at the wrists
and a brass signet ring
that sweated green,
he lounged and scratched
round the back streets,
had drinks with pimps
and the cheapest women,
a kicked-around layabout
Borstal-bred,
shiftless, lecherous,
cunning, dirty,
who now, a dear friend
of Lord Sodd
sways like a deb
from party to private party.

2

We call those women loose in spite
of thighs that clasp our own thighs tight.

3

Pretty little filly, why
do you avoid me as you do.
Perhaps you think me stupid? I
would love to bit and saddle you
and, reins held firmly in my hand,
would ride the whole long race course out,
but you prefer to trot around
the virgin meadow still, without
a skilful rider who would place
you first in the delightful race.

4

I'm in love with Cleobolus;
Cleobolus troubles me,
and I gaze on Cleobolus
perpetually.

5

You golden girl,
bright gowned in gold,
please listen to me:
I am old.

6

Love sees my beard is flecked with grey
and, golden pinioned, flies away.

7

Blacksmith Love is tempering me
again with all his skill,
first hammering then dowsing me
in the stream's winter chill.

8

You, boy, with the girlish eyes,
why do you move apart?
Do you not even realize
your reins tug at my heart?

9

For lunch I ate an oatmeal cake
and had a quart of wine,
and now I pluck the lute and sing
to this sweet maid of mine.

10

This is Timocritus' grave:
war spares the coward, not the brave.

APPOLLODOROS (6TH CENTURY BC)

Who can be creeping to my gate
now at the blackest edge of night?

ARCHILOCHUS (8TH CENTURY BC)

1

Her twin breasts and her long dark hair
were as a perfume on the air;
even old men would fall for her.

2

Dead, you don't get much respect
from anyone in your home town.
Alive, we may find favour, but
the dead get nothing more than scorn.

3

Just as the rock-borne fig-tree lets
itself be raped by long-beaked crows,
so this simple young girl gets
laid by strange men that no-one knows.

4

One only gift my prayers demand –
that I may touch Antonia's hand.

5

Some sly barbarian soldier has contrived
to steal the shield I hurled behind a bush
so hurriedly. So what! I'm still alive.
I'll indent for another, and won't blush.

6

Raise your cup on the deck of this rolling ship, drink
deep, drain all the casks, and go on drinking!
Why keep a sober watch upon this trip
since down below the whole damn crew is stinking?

DEMODOCUS (4TH CENTURY BC)

1

One time a vicious adder bit
a Cappadocian lout,
and, having merely tasted it,
immediately passed out.

2

Take one, take all –
the Turk's a jerk,
except for Paul
and Paul's a Turk.

EPICHARMUS (FL. 480 BC)

I am dust, clay, being dead,
no more than earth, but yet, consider,
if earth is, as they say, a god,
then I'm a god and no cadaver.

HEGEMON OF ALEXANDRIA (FL. 370 BC)

Gravely passing by this lettered stone
a stranger might well pause awhile and ponder
how no more than a thousand Spartan men
held back the numberless horde of Persian soldiers,
stood firm, and died, and never ran:
Such is Dorian discipline.

HIPPONAX (FL. 545 BC)

1

Never has the blind money god
come to visit me and said
"You've won the lottery; here's the loot"
He is a parsimonious brute.

2

It is an outrage. They all curse
this proper and upstanding fellow
for adultery because
they've met him there in the bordello.

3

I swear I'll steep myself in vice
if you don't quickly send me grain
so I can brew, distil, and spice
a medicine to ease my pain.

4

A woman's only truly great
on two of all her days,
the one that starts her married state,
the one on which she dies.

IBYKOS (6TH CENTURY BC)

1

Our dreaming ends as dawn skies pale
and wake the noisy nightingale.

2

Love's cast his eye on me again.
I fear that dark-browed glance
bewitching me and luring me
to Aphrodite's dance.

I tremble at the prospect as
an ageing champion horse
unwillingly once more bears colours
to the familiar course.

3

Those bare-thighed girls of Sparta
have a yen
for men, men, men, men, men,
men, men, men, men.

MIMNERMOS (FL. 600 BC)

Once man has had his day,
however much they used to love him,
all his honour drains away;
even his kids think little of him.

PERSES (4TH CENTURY BC)

Ilithyia, Goddess of
perfected children, please accept
the wedding ring and diadem
of Tisis as a thank-you gift
for safe delivery of her son;
throughout her pains she thought of them.

PHOKYLIDES (FL. 600 BC)

1

Phokylides comments "What
does all this chat of lineage matter?
Look at the blue bloods that you meet—
all bolloxed brains and vacuous chatter."

2

Fools, strolling past, attempt to ape the wise
with heads held high and supercilious eyes.

PLATO (427–348 BC)

1

Here's an apple. If you love me,
take it, girl, and then take me.
If you don't – well, take the apple.
Beauty withers. Wait and see!

2

I, Lais, who have laughed and loved,
throw out my mirror now, because
I hate the woman I've become,
and cannot find the girl I was.

3

This jasper brooch
is carved with five
small grazing cows
so much alive
you'd think that they
would scamper hence
if there were not
that golden fence.

Or alternatively

The stone of jasper is engraved
with five heifers grazing,
each looking perfectly alive;
one thinks of them escaping,
but the little herd is held
securely in a pen of gold.

4

I am a sailor's tomb, and this
a ploughman's. Friends, consider well
how under land and sea alike
exists egalitarian Hell.

5

Some aver there are nine Muses.
They should count again.
Sappho on the Isle of Lesbos
makes the number ten.

PRAXILLA (FL. 450 BC)

1

The loveliest thing I leave is sunlight,
and, after that, the radiant stars,
the gazing moon, but also ripe
green cucumbers and apples, pears.

2

Watch out! Under every stone
lurks a pincering scorpion.

3

In the window a young girl's smile
teases with bright eyes,
but out of sight I sense full well
a woman's swelling thighs.

SAPPHO (FL. 600 BC)

1

Rich, but not good, you court disaster;
if both, you are the glad world's master.

2

I cannot hope, (however high
I reach my arms), to touch the sky.

3

The good the Muses gave was golden;
dead, I shall not be forgotten.

4

Down you'll lie, and I shall lay
lovely pillows for love's body.

5

She's a choice apple flushing crimson
on the high branches farthest tip,
one that the pickers have forgotten
or found beyond their eager grasp,

or perhaps a hyacinth the shepherds
crushed in wandering the hills,
trampled, carelessly ignored,
yet purple-petalled, splendid still.

6

It was the glorious gods brought gold to birth,
made it invulnerable to worm or moth,
yet gold, the conqueror, brings destruction on
the pulse and heartbeat of the strongest man.

7

The stars around the riding moon
hide their shy faces when she sways
so near to earth as to illume
creation with a silver haze.

8

The stars are gone, the moon is down,
time dwindles and I lie alone.

9

Death is no lasting benefit,
as the gods well know
or else they would have gone for it
long long ago.

10

Were my breasts able to give suck
and womb still strong to entertain
the weight of children I would take
another husband without strain,
but now my skin is wrinkled, dry,
and Love has no desire to fly
into my arms with joy and pain.

11

It is said that Leda found
somewhere on the ground, half hidden,
and coloured like a hyacinth
one other egg she had forgotten.

12

You come again and feed my longing;
ash leaps to flame within my heart;
so here's a threefold blessing lasting
long as the years we've been apart.

13

I prayed the night I spent with you
would stretch and lengthen into two.

14

May all those that revile and curse
be torn by worry and by madness.

15

Singing, we spend all this night
to praise your loves, you happy groom
and bride as bright as violet.
Rising when the dawn has come,
may Hermes lead you on a track
where you'll encounter as much spite,
distress, disorder and bad luck
as we experience sleep tonight.

16

Where the cooling river dances
breezes, rustling through the branches
of the apple trees, caress
with quivering leaves our idleness.

17

Give up, girl. You can't rely on
bending that hard heart of iron.

18

Behind the laurel bush you stood,
and all the world grew calm and good
for we two wandering women here;
I hardly heard you come, my dear,
you were so quiet – and then this:
your sudden aching loveliness.

19

Love once more swells
my heart as gales
shake all the tall
oaks in the hills.

20

Beauty and delicacy and
all forms of loveliness are one
and fused together in my mind
like my desire for the sun.

21

In golden sandals,
Dawn, unkind
and larcenous,
has robbed me blind.

SEMONIDES OF AMORGOS (7TH CENTURY BC)

1

No man will summon
a thick-ankled woman.

2

If we were wise
we would not shed
tears more than daylong
for the dead.

SIMONIDES OF CEOS (556–467 BC)

1

You are not staring at the tall
memorial of Royalty:
I was poor; the stone is small,
and yet it overburdens me.

2

When things go right,
get tight!

SOCRATES (469–399 BC)

1

Look at me, and I look back;
you have eyes, but I have none;
you may speak, but I am speechless
for my moving lips are dumb.

2

Though I am black, my father's white;
a wingless bird, I fly from sight;
to every pupil I teach a tear,
and at my birth I turn to air.

*The solution to these two riddles are:
1. A Mirror.   2. Smoke.

SOLON (638–559 BC)

1

I will be tearless when life ends,
but hope my dying grieves my friends.

2

No man knows happiness; all men
learn misery who live beneath the sun.

STESICHOROS (630–555 BC)

Forget your tedious war stories;
it's time for song; get your guitar;
recall those girls' lubricious glories
and happy music round the bar.
The noisy swallows are on wing;
it is indubitably Spring.

THEOGNIS

1

Happy the man who has at last found out
that woman's love is but a wrestling bout
and, having won the fall, goes homeward, glad,
to sleep day out with a delicious lad.

2

Breeding stock is a matter of being careful
to get the best beasts matched with the best at stud, yet
even a sensible man will marry some dreadful
child of a dreamful man if her bank account's good.

TIMOCREON (5th century bc)

I wish that you, blind money god,
had never reached this land or sea,
but stayed beyond the Styx in Hell:
all evil comes from currency.

THUCYDIDES THE HISTORIAN (460–400 BC)

You have the whole of Greece
for tomb, so never will
that voice of yours, Euripides,
be lost or still.

TYMNES (3RD CENTURY BC)

Emelus' faithful dog lies here;
while he lived they called him Bull,
but now the noiseless paths of darkness
hold his watchful bark and howl.

XENOPHANES (565–473 BC)

Everything is born of earth
and ends up where it came to birth.

II

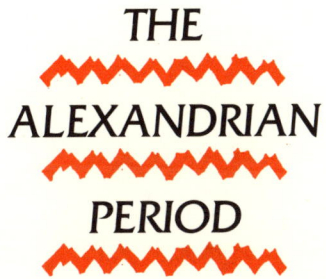

THE ALEXANDRIAN PERIOD

350 BC – 90 BC

ALKAIOS (FL. 197 BC)

1

Aristodemos told no lie when he,
one day in Sparta, said in his oration
Money Maketh Man; poor men can't be
good or gain a virtuous reputation.

2

If you say everything you want
you'll hear a good deal that you don't.

3

Strengthen your defences, Zeus –
that Philip is dead clever –
and shut those massive gates of bronze,
the bastard's taken over
land and ocean with his craft –
the road to Olympus, though, is left.

4

Unburied and unmourned we lie,
thirty thousand fighting men,
upon this hill in Thessaly
and Macedonia aches with pain
to think how noble Philip here
ran off as nimbly as a deer.

ANYTE (3RD CENTURY BC)

1

Alive, he served as slave to us;
dead, he is great as Darius.

2

Here little Philomel interred
her pet grasshopper and her bird
and then, by bitter Death bereft,
wept because her friends had left.

3

Her smooth cheeks glistening with tears,
Erato's last words to her father,
throwing her arms around his neck:
Father, I am yours no longer
I am gone; Death's darkness lies
already in your daughter's eyes.

ANTIPATER OF SIDON (2ND CENTURY BC)

1

Now is the time for seas to tear
before the running of the keel;
no longer do the waves uprear
from glistening angry chasms, while
the swallow underneath the eaves
begins to make her rounded house
and young leaves in the meadows smile;
Sailors, drag your anchors out
from their harbour hideaways
and coil the dripping hawsers in;
haul high the sail: for so commands
Priapus, holy harbour king.

2

This is Anacreon's grave. Here lie
the shreds of his exuberant lust,
but hints of perfume linger by
his gravestone still, as if he must
have chosen for his last retreat
a place perpetually on heat.

ARISTON

If you mice want first class nosh
you'd better leave my shack,
for almost anywhere's more posh –
I'm broke. Trot off and snack
on dried figs, camembert and brie –
that's fine, but if you nibble
just one page in my library,
Mice, you'll be in trouble.

ASCLEPIADES (320–275 BC)

1

Why must you keep your maidenhead
until the bitter end? Once dead,
no man will make your bedsprings groan.

Only the living can have fun.
Die – and what have we become
but lonely heaps of ash and bone?

2

It's wonderful to suck ice
in a sweltering summer,
and marvellous after a blizzard
to feel the still
candour of air, but triumphant
when two young lovers
lie under one coat, warm
on an April hill.

3

The winter nights are long. The sun
goes down before the stars are born.
I pass, repass, and haunt her door,
drenched, chilled, and shaken by the storm,
and feverish with desire for her,
the cheating bitch; and if I tell
you this is love, I lie – it's more
the madness of a living hell.

4

Cleo's beauty makes me burn
with longing; it consumes and slays!
You sneer and say her skin is black?
Coals bloom to roses when they blaze!

ASKLEPIADES (4TH CENTURY BC)

1

Jane bit me! I admit it doesn't show,
but pain creeps through me to my fingers, chilling
every inch; I'm finished, drained, wiped out;
the girl's a viper and her kiss is killing.

2

As I felt pretty Julia up
I noticed that she wore
a belt with letters made of gems;
the message that it bore
said very clearly, "Love me quick,
but don't get cross or blue
when you discover, as you will,
that I screw others, too."

3

Drink up, Asklepiades!
Why tears? What has occurred?
You're not the only one that she's
treated as a nerd.
Love's narrowed eyes
take constant aim
and many are hard hit;
but they survive it all the same.
There's no need to eat shit.

4

The Pleiades have almost set;
outside her house, bedraggled, wet,
I burn, I ache and shake and twitch –
but it is lust, not love – the bitch!

5

Wine is one of love's best tests;
John swears he has no lover,
but after several cheerful toasts
his bleary eyes run over
and the wreath upon his brow
slides anywhere and anyhow.

6

Kypris, Kleo offers you
this little golden spur
she wore upon her ankle to
urge lovers on who were
enchanted by such discipline,
though her thighs never bore
a scratch; her riding days are done
so this hangs on your door.

ANTIPATER OF THESSALONICA

I am Drunkenness engraved
upon a sober amethyst
quite inappropriately, I'd say,
but I'm on Cleopatra's fist,
the ring of that immortal queen,
and since I am thus owned,
although a goddess, I've not been
entitled to get stoned.

CALLIMACHUS (300–240 BC)

1

This stony sepulchre you pass is
now the tomb of Callimachus;
he could sing and he could laugh
while the red wine filled the glasses.

Or alternatively

This is the grave of Battos' son
who had some skill in composition
and knew the right time to combine
his laughter with the circling wine.

2

Timon, since you're dead at last,
inform me which you most detest,
the darkness or the light. Please tell.
The dark, for there are more like you in Hell.

3

They tell me, Heraclitus,
that you've died,
and I remember clearly
as I mourn,
how long we talked together
side by side
until the gentle evening
sun went down,

but now, my friend,
you lie somewhere unknown,
and are no more than a
small box of dust,
and yet your nightingales
live on and on
untouched by Death
who's taken all the rest.

CRATES (4TH CENTURY BC)

1

Hunger puts an end to love,
and if hunger cannot tame
your passions, Time will quickly dowse
the fury of the amorous flame:
if, spite of these, your pains endure,
then suicide's the only cure.

Or alternatively

One of the cures for love is hunger
another remedy is time;
but if you cannot bear to linger
there is the hangman's noose and lime.

CRINAGORAS (1ST CENTURY BC)

Whether you toss this way or that in bed,
switch from right side to left, or left to right,
makes little odds, my friend, for if your head
is not beside Estella's through the night
you'll get no proper sleep, but harassed, worn,
will wake, played out, in an exhausted dawn.

DIONYSIUS OF ANDROS

Soaked to the skin by Zeus' rain
and Bacchus' booze, I slipped and fell,
and that's no wonder – two to one
are bad enough, but Gods as well?

DIONYSIUS OF HERACLEA

A time to love,
a time to wed,
a time to lie
long in the bed.

DIONYSIUS THE SOPHIST

You, yes, you with the chocolates –
You're pretty enough to eat,
yourself! Are you selling yourself,
or the chocolates, or both, my sweet?

DIOSCORIDES (3RD CENTURY BC)

1

I'm crazy about those
red murmuring lips
whose kisses drive me wild,
those passionate eyes
beneath the bold dark brows,
those full-curved breasts
that bring delirium –
but I'll be wise:
no names, no pack-drill –
why should I go on
to tell you sniffing dogs
where good meat lies?

2

If Julian, when he grows up, gives
the sort of kiss he now hands out,
while still a child, to those he loves,
his mother's doorbell will wear out!

3

John's ancient nurse,
who would drink deep
and long of wine
now lies asleep
within the vineyard;
may her bones
feed well the vats
she treasured once.

DIOTIMOS (or possibly leonidas)

In dusk the beasts plod home through snow,
drift by themselves into their byre,
their cowherd in death's sleep below
an oak tree felled by heaven's fire.

HEDYLUS (FL. 270 BC)

1

Of Drink, that loosener of tongues,
and Love that loosens clothes and thighs,
a child is born; see where she comes,
Miss Gout, loose-limbed until she dies.

2

Drink up! Wine provides the tongue
with such a copious play of wit
who knows what I may hit upon?
Give me another jug of it,
and cry, "Hedylus, drink!" for I
am wasting time by staying dry.

LEONIDAS OF TARENTUM (3RD CENTURY BC)

1

I am a stone on Cretho's head,
and spell his name who shares this earth
with other ashes, who was once
renowned as Gyges for his wealth
and rich with herds of goats – but why
talk further? He whom all thought glad
has now so small a portion of
the countless acres that he had.

2

Jack, the cattle farmer, flayed
the mountain lion that he killed
as it attacked the staggering calf;
no longer can it have its will
with jostling sheep and hurry back
to forest safety. It has paid
the murdered calf in blood for blood
and mourns the outcome of its raid.

3

Myron swears he's carved me, but
the man's a liar; all he's done
is drive me from my grazing herd
and glue me to a base of stone.

4

Here is Krito's tiny hut;
here's his little patch of corn,
his small stack of kindling wood,
and the wee tangle of the vine
he loved so terribly, and here's
where he spent eighty happy years.

5

I'm Tellen's tomb; beneath this earth
lies the progenitor of mirth
who brought the comic song to birth.

6

Eubolus? Remember him?
Teetotal all his days.
Here's his grave. Let's have a drink.
We all end the same place.

MELEAGER (1ST CENTURY BC)

1

Dawn, you spoilsport, why on earth
are you so long in coming when
another man's tucked up beneath
Estella's sheet, for, once again,
you were so quick to end the fun
when I embraced her naked there
that, long before we'd really done,
we paled to feel your gleeful stare.

2

The claret quivers as it feels
the slow caress of Helen's lips,
those amorous thieves that gently steal
away its lifeblood as she sips,
and makes me envious of the cup
that, for her kisses, drains its bowl;
if only she would take me up,
and, kissing, suck away my soul!

3

By Gloria's blonde unravelled hair
that shakes like waters to her passion;
by Helen's breasts that banish sleep;
By Jane's elaborate persuasions;
and by the lamp that for so long
has gaped upon our games, I swear
to you, Love, though I've not much breath
left in my weary bones, I'll spare
you that as well: if you should doubt,
just give the sign – I'll pant it out!

4

Helen, who's in love with love,
whose eyes are blue as seas offshore
from Paradise, persuades all men
to ride her depths with dripping oar.

5

Love shaped Eve's crimson fingernail
with more than mortal art,
for even its most gentle scratches
rake into my heart.

6

Hop away, my little flea,
and take a message to my dear.
Skip into her bed and be
a conscience whispering in her ear.

Murmur someone that adores
her madly, lies awake, that he
is racked with anguish as she snores.
Hop away, my little flea,

But, oh, be careful. Do not shout
in case her husband hears you too,
and finds our little secret out.
You know what jealous husbands do!

But, if you can, persuade my dear
to steal away from him to me.
Suggest it sweetly in her ear.
Be a cunning little flea.

And if she comes, I'll see you get
a great big club, and you shall be
wrapped in a lionskin, my pet;
so hop away, you little flea.

7

I'm out of love with Gerald, and
though Julian once burned bright as fire,
he's now a burned-out faggot, so
these days it's women I desire —
for no one but a goatherd feasts
his love upon such hairy beasts!

8

Darkness, wakeful hours that long
for her dear company, then dawn
tormented with remembered tears,
remembered happiness; I turn

in fevered sheets to ponder what
is left of everything we had:
do my kisses still feel warm
upon her in her dreaming bed?

Does she sleep with only tears
for loving company, and slip
her arms around her absent lover,
kissing his imagined lips?

Or has she got another man?
Oh, may this lamp I send her see
no stranger there, but guard her well
and keep her warm and dear for me.

9

If I should die, friend – and I burn
already, and am almost ash
for love of boys – then fill my urn
with claret: let it swirl and splash
until it's drunk before you let
them bed it down. And, when you shove
the wreath on top, write on the stone,
"This present comes to Death from Love."

10

Why have you left the flower-beds
you busy petal-nuzzling bee,
and settle on Diana's skin?
Do you mean to hint that she

not only is the sweetest girl
but also knows the way to sting
so sharply that it hurts the heart?
If that's the message that you bring,

buzz off, get lost, skedaddle, blow!
Or tell me something I don't know.

11

The rose in Janet's hair has shed
its freshness and is almost dead,
but Janet with such beauty glows
the woman now adorns the rose.

12

Dark waves of love, where are you taking me
on sleepless winds of turbulent jealousy,
climactic roaring seas? Without a rudder
I drift, directionless. Oh, will I see
ever again the soft shores of my lover?

13

Your eyes are fire to me, my sweet;
your touch is bird-lime to my feet.
I'm burning, on heat at your look,
and if you touch me I'll be stuck.

MNASALKES (3RD CENTURY BC)

You crossed the Styx still young, unwed;
only the tears your mother shed
support her now as she lies weeping
on the stone above your head.

NOSSIS (FL. 275 BC)

Let's go to Aphrodite's temple,
see her statue wrought in gold.
Polyarchis the beautiful
provided it because she owed
it to the Goddess out of duty,
having herself grown rich on beauty.

PHALAIKOS (FL. 300 BC)

Kleo gives to Dionysus
this her yellow gold-hemmed gown
decks his statue with her dress
because for all her life she shone
at every party and there were
no men could drink as deep as her.

PHILLIP V OF MACEDON (238–179 BC)

Traveller on this hillside, look,
and see a bare and crooked cross,
a tree with neither leaf nor bark
and learn it's here to say Alkaios.

PHILITAS (330–270 BC)

1

Nikias, who lived for love,
now played out, in her fiftieth year,
has given to the temple of
great Aphrodite all her gear –
the cunning sandals that enflamed,
the mirror in which she could see
all loveliness, those strange unnamed
devices men might never see,
and all of passion's panoply.

2

This tombstone tells,
weighed down by grief,
Death stole this little
girl's wee life.
The girl herself
tells her dear Dad
We all have bad luck.
Don't be sad.

POSIDIPPUS (310 BC–?)

1

Don't think you kid me, Janice, with those tears.
I know the score. You love me most of all
so long as we're in bed together here.
Once you're with someone else my stock will fall.

2

If she's with someone I'll not fret her,
but if she's sleeping on her own
open up the door and let her
know I staggered here, alone
and stoned, with danger on each side,
and that Love's courage was my guide.

THEODORIDAS (3RD CENTURY BC)

The hunting stars disturbed the sea
which vomited upon the rocks
this hideous thousand-footed beast
whose giant rib the Masters of
the equally huge galleys lodge
here in homage to the gods.

THEOKRITOS (308–240 BC)

Traveller, gaze upon this stone,
the statue of Anakreon,
and then, when you are back at home,
tell how you set your eyes upon
the greatest master of pure song
who used his life to please the young.

ZENODOTOS

Who was it sculpted Love and stood
the statue by the fountain here?
Did he believe that water could
diminish or control that fire?

III

THE
ROMAN
PERIOD

90 BC – AD 50

ADDAEUS OF MACEDON (1ST CENTURY AD)

John spared his patient labouring ox,
worn out by years and the plough,
the answer of the bloody axe,
and thanked it for its service; now,
somewhere, half-lost in meadow grass,
it lows in soft requited ease,
glad of the respite from the plough,
rejoicing in release.

ANTIPATOR

Now I am dead and I belong
neither to the ocean nor
the land, my flesh consumed by fish,
my bones cast up on the cold shore.

ANTIPATER OF THESSALONICA
(FL. 20 BC–AD 20)

1

Astrologers foretold to me
I'd live till I was thirty-six,
but I will settle for the three
decades and then be glad to quit,
for thirty years is the proper
limit of our mortal span;
Nestor may have lasted longer,
but he went to Hades then!

2

She's lovely as Europa. For ten bucks
with none to stop you, and no opposition
on her part, but rather the reverse,
you can have her. She's in good condition,
and takes care; her sheets are always clean;
she lights a fire if the day is cool.
A mere ten bucks. There was no reason, Zeus,
to make a thing of it with all that bull!

3

When the deep-piled winter snow
melted on her roof, it caved
the timbers in and killed her, but
her neighbours did not make a grave;
they left her in her friendly room,
her tomb her home, her home a tomb.

4

No battle or typhoon or tremor
fills me with such mortal terror
as this water drinker who
observes us mopping up the brew
and, listening with flapping ears,
remembers everything he hears.

ANTIPHANES

Cythera gave her sash
to Ino, granting her the luck
to snare all men she wished, bewitch
and break their hearts. So Ino took
the sash and now I find she's thrown
its noose round me and me alone.

ARCHIAS (1st century ad)

1

Not much to look at, I agree!
Yet I, Priapus, lacking feet,
and with a dome for head, set up
on this promontory by the beach,

companion of the wheeling gulls
and creatures of both sea and land,
though crude as any carving made
by fisher boys upon the sand,

fly swifter than the wind when called
to help a man with net or rod,
and know all secrets of the deep:
the character of any god

lies not within the shapes he takes
but in the miracles he makes.

2

Apelles surely must have seen
the nursing sea deliver Cypris
to draw her thus, with newmade hands
still wringing water from her tresses.

3

Run from Eros?
What's the use?
There is no hope
of an escape
on human feet
from one so fleet
upon the wing
close-following.

AUTOMEDON (1st century bc)

1

Yesterday I ate tough mutton
and a cabbage ten days old;
I won't say where I went for dinner,
for my host is of a cold
revengeful temper, and he might
invite me back another night.

2

Each evening when we drink together
we are men; but each new day
we wake and rise to rend each other,
savage, ravening beasts of prey.

BASSUS (1ST CENTURY AD)

1

I'll never change myself to gold.
Other fools that want can make
themselves into big-chested bulls,
or swans that honk across the lake.
I leave such tricks to them and Zeus.
Why play at birds when I can see
here in my hand ten willing bucks
to pay Joyce for an entrance fee?

2

When the Father of the Shades
saw three hundred newly dead,
all battle-slain, a second time,
"These men are Spartans all" he said.
"Look! Every wound is, as before,
in front, and not a scratch behind.
Great Warriors, cease this thirst for blood,
and learn, with us, the quiet mind."

BIANOR (1ST CENTURY AD)

1

Duck-hunter, seeking reed-beds out,
be very careful! Do not take
the forest paths on naked feet;
avoid the little grey-eyed snakes,

and watch your every step. Look out
in case you, hurrying on your path
to shoot the creatures of the air,
are poisoned by the secret earth.

2

In the clear water by the beach
an octopus was swimming, and
a fisherman, who saw it, grabbed
and threw it high upon the land,

afraid his prey might trap him if
he wasn't careful. There it flailed
its tentacles and writhed until
it happened on a timorous wild

half-sleeping hare among the reeds,
and strangled it. Thus, all unplanned,
the fisherman's sea-plunder brought
him further plunder on the land.

3

When this house fell
it crushed and killed
all in its walls
except a child;
on him it tumbled
gentler than
the mildest breeze,
as if the ruin
pitied infants
and the stones
recalled their mothers'
labouring groans.

ERYCIUS (1ST CENTURY BC)

I, the priest of Rhea, long-haired
castrato, Tmolian dancer, whose
high shriek is famed for carrying power,
now, at last, rest from my throes

and give the Great Dark Mother on
the banks of the Sangarius all:
my tambourines, my bone-linked scourge,
my brazen cymbals, and a curl

of my long heavy perfumed hair
in dedication, Holy Rhea.

EVENUS OF ASCALON

Though you gnaw me to the root,
old billy goat, I'll manage fruit
and wine enough to do my bit
when your skinny throat is slit.

GAETULICUS (?–AD 39)

Here upon the seashore Archilochus
lies in death and will not rise again.
His muse was vicious, viperous;
Mount Helicon he smeared and stained
with blood, and, pierced by his abuse,
the Graces hung themselves for shame.
Tread softly, stranger, lest you stir
the wasps that keep their dwelling there.

HONESTUS (1ST CENTURY AD)

1

The very day one son was drowned
she lit the other's funeral pyre;
two griefs, two gifts, destroyed her heart,
one given water, and one fire.

2

I would not wed a young girl or old woman;
from reverence and pity love retreats.
I don't want juiceless grape or wrinkled raisin
but full ripe beauty for my bridal sheets.

ISIDORUS SCHOLASTICUS

Now Endymion dedicates
his cold bed's failure to the moon,
for grey hair frosts his ageing head
and all his beauty is long gone.

MAECIUS (1st century AD)

Angela, that cruel bitch
who's never ever gone around
with anyone not filthy rich
appears at last to have reformed.

This is miraculous, if true,
but I can't swallow miracles;
the viper may look gentle, too,
but when it kisses you, it kills.

MARCUS ARGENTARIUS (1st century AD)

1

As I read *The Decline and Fall*
Jane wandered into sight and mind;
I slung the book against the wall
and left it fallen and declined.

2

Well, Jim, you once were rich and found
yourself in love; now you are poor,
and Joyce, who loved the very ground
you trod on, visits you no more,
but, out at parties, asks your name
from friends, pretends you've never met.
It's rough – but it's all in the game.
Nothing Have means Nothing Get.

3

Take those dark glasses off, Lucille,
They tease too much. And let your hips
roll less provocatively, for
the way that clinging satin slips
and slides on buttocks and on breasts
suggests the nakedness it hides
so clearly that you seem both stripped
and dressed at once. To be so eyed
by all the men may give you kicks,
but if you don't give up I swear
I'll take to clothes like that, half show,
Half hide a thing to make *you* stare!

4

Dead, you'll huddle six feet under,
far from the day and joys of life,
so drink deep friend. No need to ponder.
Make love to your lovely wife,
don't think immortal wisdom's on the way;
the sages also lie deep in the clay.

5

You, like your namesake, Bea, love flowers,
and your warm kiss is moist with honey,
but also, you know how to sting
your lover with demands for money.

6

Let go the mooring hawsers, spread
your easy sails, set out to sea,
Captain, for the storms are done
and little breezes laughingly
make oceans gentle as a girl;
already the maternal swallow
moulds its home of mud and straw
with whispering beak, and in the hollow
of the pasture flowers spring;
listen, therefore, to the god
Priapus, and take heart to go
on any voyage you are bid.

7

In love with young Elaine, at last
I talked her into it! We played
together, breathless, in my room;
our hearts were thumping, and, afraid
that someone might surprise our love,
we talked in whispers, but we had
been overheard – her Mother's face
poked round the bedroom door and said:
"No cheating, now! Remember, Dear,
We share and share alike round here!"

MYRINUS (1st century ad)

When Time was all prepared to drag
that Nancy, that old screaming queer,
off down to Hades, he minced out
and gave Priapus all his gear –
the greasy perfumed wig, the pairs
of high heels, and the little box
in which he kept his falsie spares:
he even gave the flute that played
sweet music to his fellow maids.

PARMENION

Danae was paid in gold
for suffering love's abuse;
here's one gold coin; when all is told
I do no more than Zeus.

PHILODEMUS (1ST CENTURY BC)

1

I slipped my wary husband's leash
and came to you, although the rain
of midnight drenched me to the skin,
and now, together once again
to talk and lie together, why
do we not talk, and kiss, and lie?

2

Common sense tells me to leave
Estella flat; it knows so well
the jealousies and tantrums that
have in the past made love a hell:
but I can't make it. Though the bitch
herself insists it would be wise,
she does so as our bodies touch,
and warns with kisses and with sighs.

3

Jane is petite, a neat brunette,
her small head piled with glistening curls,
her white skin smooth, her pouting breasts
both firm and soft; the darling girl
grants every joy a man can have,
is glad at each small gift I get her:
Gods, may I always keep her love –
or, leastways, till I get a better.

4

I fell in love with a cute blonde called Ann
at Whitstable – there's nothing odd in that;
but then another Ann in London took
my fancy – nothing yet to wonder at;
but Ann of Leeds was next, and that seemed strange;
and then the fourth that let me act the man
was Ann as well: by name and nature both
I'm Andrew – I've been always drawn to Ann.

5

At sixty, Juliette's mass of hair
is black as it has ever been;
she needs no brassiere to uplift
and firm her marble breasts; her skin
is still unwrinkled, perfumed, quick
to welcome and provoke desire:
so, if you're bold enough to face
love's fiercest, most enduring fire,
call Juliette, and have no fears –
you'll soon forget those sixty years!

6

Jim gives his Barbara twenty bucks
just for the once, yet is afraid
and shakes with guilt. I give Ginette
a single five; for that she's laid
a good round dozen times, and she's
the prettier girl, and doesn't care
a jot who knows what games we play.
Now, do you think I'm nuts to swear
Jim's one of those whose future life
would gain from the castrating knife?

PINYTOS (FL. AD 50)

The grave holds Sappho's
bones and name,
but her wise deathless
words remain.

STATYLLIUS FLACCUS (1ST CENTURY BC/AD)

1

I am a shaded lamp, a gift
from Anthony to Dorothy
beside whose shaking bed I lift
a flame that almost dies to see
her indiscriminate affairs,
while he that called us both his own
so recently, like me burns out,
but disregarded and alone.

2

At last, on Julian's peach-bloom cheek
that turned from lovers in disgust
the hairs are sprouting, and he's fallen
for a boy! The Fates are just!

Or, alternatively

Julian, who's begun to grow
a beard has always told us "No,"
but now a boy's aroused his lust:
Nemesis is quick and just!

DIODORUS ZONAS

Give this right hand a foaming pot
fired from the dark life-giving clay
we come from, and, when we are not,
lie under till the Judgement Day.

IV

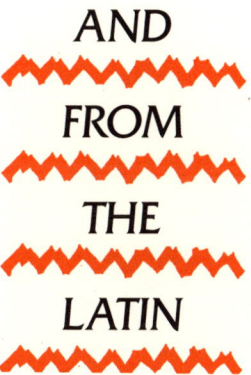

PACUVIUS (220 BC–130 BC)

Don't hurry off; look at this stone;
consider what the words imply.
Pacuvius, the poet, has gone.
I thought you'd like to know. Goodbye.

SULPICIA (FL. 25 BC)

Don't you feel pity for your love, Cerinthis,
now as fever trembles her weak frame?
I'd have no desire to conquer illness
if I thought your desire were not the same.
This fight to win's no good and makes no sense
if you survey it with indifference.

HORACE (65 BC–8 BC)

1

Why, Chloe, do you run from me
as if a timid faun, alarmed
by high winds whistling in a tree,
scampering to her doe for calm?

In the chilly dawn of Spring
leaves may tremble, lizards make
a stray twig snap, and, shivering,
young hearts may thump and small knees shake,

but I'm no lion or tiger, dear,
intent to stalk and pounce and rend,
and you're too grown to have such fear;
you must leave mother in the end.

2

It isn't sensible, my friend,
to fret at what the gods have planned
for you or me, our destined end;
tell your astrologer to go hang!
Take troubles as they come, and let
Jove work the business out. This year
that starts with winds and storms and wet
may be our last. While we chat here
old age comes closer. Challenge it!
Drink deep life's wine and throw away
those long defeated hopes. Don't sit
still till tomorrow; live today!

HADRIAN (AD 76–AD 138)

O spirit, tiny feather, cloud,
my body's comrade and wee guest,
naked pale and stiff and pallid
where now have you run to rest,
and do you still play games and jest?

PETRONIUS (FL. AD 66)

In this helmet, warm, at rest,
doves have made themselves a nest
incontrovertibly to prove
Mars is Venus' dearest love.

CATULLUS (84 BC–54 BC)

1

Okay, I'll bugger you and suck you off
Aurelius, Furius, you pansy two
who think because my verses are so rough
that I've no sexual inhibitions too.
Though poets, being sacred, should abstain from lust
it doesn't follow that their verses must.

2

Since you're behind the bar tonight
make this one really stiff;
Postumia approves alright –
she's juiced as a grape herself.
That water can piss anywhere;
it screws booze; pack it off
to the bluenose and the sober.
This is the real good stuff!

3

I love her and detest her;
you ask me to explain?
I haven't any answer;
I only have the pain.

4

You there, with the
hardly minuscule snozzle,
feet not exactly small
and unlovely eyes,
fingers that no-one could
call slim or tapering,
and a mouth that must be
admitted is rarely dry,
not forgetting a tongue
that's always protruding –
you, who bed with that
big slob of a bankrupt,
people in the suburbs
praise you plenty,
compare you to my
Lesbia. How inept!
what an uncivilized
disgusting country!

5

She wants only me, none other,
not even Jove, or so she raves;
what a woman tells her lover
write on the wind, write on the waves.

6

You've got me down so
absolutely, Lesbia,
my heart has self-destructed
from serving you
and cannot love you
however well you behave,
nor cease to love you
whatever fool thing you do.

7

You, Lesbia's pretty sparrow
that she fondles in her lap,
offering you her finger tips,
your pecking quick and sharp,

when fired up with my desire
she loves this game; I guess
when love disturbs her with its heat
you soothe her restlessness.

Sparrow, if we could play like her
I too might cope with my despair.

8

Lesbia, the beloved of Catullus,
Lesbia, Lesbia, whom he loves much more
even than his own self and his pleasures
now cruises all the narrow streets and alleys
and fucks young horny Romans like a whore.

MARTIAL (AD 43–AD 104)

1

You want to marry him – that's no surprise –
you're wise to want, and he (who won't) is wise.

2

Say "No," my love, say "No," for your delaying
satisfaction makes my love more strong,
but, darling, have a care! Don't go on saying
"No" too long.

3

You only praise dead poets. Forgive me if
I think the price of praise extremely stiff.

4

Whoever thinks his morning breath is stinking
with last night's wine just doesn't know the form;
when this one starts to drink he goes on drinking
until dawn.

5

You were her husband. Now she is your ex —
and has remarried you've become her lover.
Why do you take such trouble to annex
her once again and gain more pleasure over
her these days than when you both were one?
Do you need obstacles to turn you on?

6

She swears that no-one beds her without pay.
It's true. Her lovers earn their bread that way.

7

If you are poor then poor you'll surely stay;
only the wealthy get well paid today.

8

You want me always at full stretch for you —
my dear, sometimes there's no string to the bow!
However much your words and touch cry "Do,"
your face incontrovertibly calls "No!"

9

I praised his book in print, and yet he's treating
me as if he didn't know. That's cheating!

10

Her seven husbands' tombs spell out
the candid sentence "Chloe fecit,"
which leaves no room for any doubt;
it's true, whatever way you take it.

11

"I bought a plot of land the other day –
lend me a thousand, will you – I am broke!"
You hesitate. You think I might not pay.
Quite frankly, that's the reason that I spoke.

12

She always has a tiny tot
around her skirts and she delights
in calling it her pet, her sweet,
though she detests the little mites.
You ask me why? It plays the part
of culprit when she has to fart.

13

That suit cost him a thousand bucks or more.
It's custom tailored, not from any store,
and it's a bargain! What is that you say?
Why so? It's obvious. He'll never pay.

14

First married, you denied he was your lover,
but when you married him you blew your cover!

15

If you can spare the time, read this.
You've not a damn thing else to do
and yet you give my verse a miss!
Percipient you!

16

Dressed up in the latest style,
you see my threadbare suit and smile.
It may be shabby, I admit,
but (unlike some) I've paid for it.

17

You ask why I won't marry you?
You're too much of a prude,
and I am sure that you would view
all bedroom games as rude.

18

Young Camilla tries to look more old;
ancient Gellia calls herself a girl;
both are ridiculous; when all is told
no sane man would give either one a whirl.

19

So modest, reticent and good,
how did you manage fatherhood?

20

His rhymes condemn me, but I do not heed them.
He's no true writer; nobody can read them.

21

She boasted of her great descent,
foresaw her wedding as resplendent,
even royal. Then she went
and married a gas pump attendant.

22

Your wife's a grasping skinflint it is said;
untrue; she'll give to anyone in bed.

23

Since, Darling, I can't meet your price
why don't you simply say "No dice!"

24

Her female friends have all departed life;
I wish that she were friendly with my wife.

25

You ask me why his ear smells like shit?
Because you're always whispering in it.

26

In purchasing my house, this longtime guest
is only paying for what he has possessed.

27

We bathed, we feasted, full of fun.
But the next morning he lay dead.
You ask me why his dying was so sudden?
He dreamed of Dr. Pillbox by his bed.

28

Do not despise this little gift of mine;
that vinegar was worse when it was wine.

29

Some of my epigrams are grand,
some only fair, some simply suck;
my friend, I hope you understand
this is the way one fills a book.

30

Your pet dog licks your mouth and lips
as you caress him on your lap;
I do not wonder why, for it's
a doggy habit to eat crap.

31

Phidias carved these fish;
all praise to him;
put them in water and
I swear they'll swim.

32

I am your heir, Catullus, you have said.
I won't believe it till the will is read.

33

I don't send you my books? Of course!
I'm scared that you might send me yours.

V

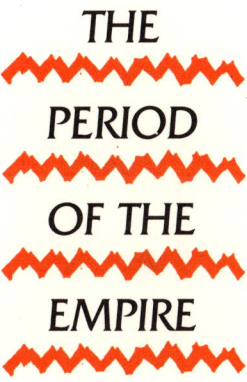

THE PERIOD OF THE EMPIRE

AD 50 – AD 450

AMMIANUS (2ND CENTURY AD)

1

You think that beard has made you wise,
but "Cut it off" is my advice;
that goatish fly-swat is the cause,
not of your learning, but your lice.

2

John's efforts to extract a thorn
failed miserably. He was so thin
that when the pin approached his foot
it was the foot that pierced the pin.

3

It's not the way you suck a sugar stick
that makes you someone that I cannot stand,
it is the way you also suck and lick
when you have got no sugar stick to hand.

4

Dawn follows dawn it seems for ever,
then suddenly, all dawns have stopped –
dropsy, consumption, gout and fever,
a hole in earth, and earth on top.

AMMONIDES

If we had showed them naked Joan
our enemies would all have flown.

ANTIPHILUS OF BYZANTIUM (1ST CENTURY AD)

1

I took his dripping corpse upon
my dolphin back and reached the sand;
the beast played saviour to the man;
the sea thing saved the thing of land;

the living helped the dead. And yet
it did me little good: I left
the water for the earth and got
my death as payment for my gift

of ferry-service. He and I
changed destinies: my friendly sea
destroyed him who was of the land,
and his earth proved the end of me.

2

Nearing home at last, I said
"Tomorrow this contrary wind
that's battered me so long will drop."
The words had scarcely made their sound

when hell broke lose upon the sea,
and my careless thought had spilled
complete destruction on my head.
Oh, never say, "Tomorrow will . . ."

for Fate observes the smallest thing
and hates the over-sanguine tongue.

3

When she was still an infant, sweet
and innocent, I swore she would
grow up to set the town on heat,
but nobody believed she could.

Now, however, I'm proved right.
Each man that sees her feels the pain,
myself included; love's delight
and hunger ravish me again,

each glimpse of her excites me so;
not seeing her is just as bad; it
hurts all ways, for she says No
and plays the virgin. Chums, we've had it!

APPOLLINARIUS

Revile me secretly, I'm not annoyed,
but praise me to my face and I'm destroyed.

CILLACTOR

1

Girls are a tasty dish, agreed,
but once they ask for money
my taste-bud withers and they seem
more vinegar than honey.

2

A girl grows rich, not by her arts
but simply by her natural parts.

CALLICTER

Though Doctor Pillbox never called
to physic me or feel my side,
in bed with fever, I recalled
his name, and died.

CAPITO

Artless beauties don't disturb;
they are the bait without the barb.

CLAUDIANUS

This snow-white crystal ball
that man has fashioned shows
the various image of the whole
and flawless universe,
the heavens clasping endlessly
the deep reverberance of the sea.

CYRILLUS

Epigrams? Two lines, no more.
Three, they're epics and a bore.

DEMOCRITUS

When Cypris, long hair drenched with foam,
rose naked from the vivid tide
she clasped the hair that brushed her cheeks
and with her wringing fingers dried
it of the salt Aegean flood,
revealing openly her breasts,
as women may: if she's this good,
to Hell with Ares' jealous fret!

DIOGENES LAERTIUS (3RD CENTURY AD)

1

Nor, by God, shall we neglect
to tell how this one died of gout,
however curious it may seem
that he, who used to get about
by using other people's feet,
could suddenly become so well
that in the space of one short night
he scampered all the way to Hell.

2

This is the island Salamis
that broke the insolent Medes in war,
the first home and now burial place
of Solon, maker of the law.

DIOPHANES OF MYRINA

A double-dyed thief,
that's Love I swear,
arriving boldly by night
and stripping us bare.

EVODUS

Echo:
      mimic,
last sip
of the heard wine,
word's tip.

FRONTO

As actor you think you are at your best
in *Love for Love*, but that play's had its day.
Soon you'll be playing in *Love's Labour's Lost*,
then, season following season, you will say
that *Hamlet* is the tragedy to stage,
and, later, *Lear* you feel will suit you most
as you accept the fantasies of age,
concluding with a minor part in *Ghosts*.

GEMINUS (1st century ad)

Its plinth alone prevents this bronze
young heifer getting up to go.
Unanchor it and it would run
to join the herd. Just hear it low!
The sculptor made it so alive
that I am sure if one more cow
were yoked beside it, they would both
prove excellent workers at the plough.

GLAUCUS (2ND OR 3RD CENTURY AD)

1

There was a time when I could lure
a young lad with a spinning top;
now, however, they ask cash,
and I must sigh and let it drop.

2

Neither earth nor heavy gravestone
form Erasippus' tomb
but the whole vast span of ocean,
for he and his fine ship went down
to death together; where he fell
only the seagulls know to tell.

GLYCON

Dust, laughter, nothingness: our all
is born of the nonsensical.

SAINT GREGORY THE THEOLOGIAN
(4TH CENTURY AD)

1

This fisher, netted like a fish,
in being trapped escaped life's mesh.

2

Why do you heave apart my stone?
The feeble dead are all I own;
my wealth is nothing more than bone.

3

Leave my tomb. Employ your pick
upon your cabbage patch instead,
for I have nothing in my pit
but the watchful angry dead.

IRENAEUS REFERENDARIUS (6TH CENTURY AD)

Why, Darling, do you bend your head,
look at the floor, and flush, and play
games with your necklace? Nothing's wrong
with making love! If you won't say
"Yes" out aloud, you won't; but why
not drop a hint that I may *try*?

JULIAN THE APOSTATE (AD 332–363)

He's two and she is four feet tall,
so when upon their bed they rest,
both pairs of feet against the wall,
imagine where his mouth is pressed.

LEONIDAS OF ALEXANDRIA (1ST CENTURY AD)

1

We oxen are not only good
at cutting furrows with the plough,
but excellent at hauling ships
up from the sea to land; we know
the oarsman's trade as well as that
of ploughman; therefore, sea, command
your dolphins to be just as deft
and yoke them up to work the land.

2

You send me reams of snowy paper,
and elegant Egyptian pens;
Dionysus, do not offer
poets imperfect gifts again
but use your head! Consider! Think!
What use are these without some ink!

LUCIAN (2ND CENTURY AD)

1

As everyone got stinking, Jack
decided to stay sober,
and all agreed from how he spoke
he must be half seas over.

2

Although the wicked thing you do
may well be hidden from a man, it
can't be hidden from the gods,
though all that you have done is plant it.

3

All that mortal man possesses
has mortality and passes;
everything goes hurrying past
or is passed by us at last.

4

None has seen the Paphian bare,
but if one did, it was the rare
Praxiteles who sculptured her.

5

At five years old and rarely sad,
Death took me off, a wee young lad;
my little life should cause no sadness –
I saw but little of its badness.

6

Wisdom consists
in letting your beard grow?
So you insist
my billy goat's read Plato?

LUCILIUS (1ST CENTURY AD)

1

Eye-shadow, lipstick, powder, cream,
mascara, hair-dye, dentures; Grace
has spent so much that it would seem
for less she could have bought a face.

2

Ancient Jane, who's dyed her hair
from white to black, still plays the fool;
she's suddenly so young, we stare,
not on a girl, but on a ghoul.

3

Drusilla's hired her son a tutor
who's so keen upon his functions
that he stays each night to teach her
new declensions and conjunctions.

4

That raven gloss on Cleo's head they swear
was born of Mother Bottle, but they lie;
the colour must be natural, for that hair
was quite the most expensive she could buy.

5

Her's must be a special mirror
made to beautify and soften;
if it told the truth she'd never
want to gaze in it so often.

6

When migraine troubles Tom he smells
not smelling salts but dollar bills.

7

John with a needle probed his toe;
his toe went through the needle, though.

8

Lazy Larry dreamed one night
he ran a race, and ever after
never slept a wink in case
he dreamed again of running faster.

9

If I for one second think
of Professor Deadwright's grammar,
straight away my tongue grows thick
and I start to spit and stammer.

10

Thin Jimmy, blowing trumpet, blew
so hard he blew himself right through.

11

Though Artist John had twenty sons
he never got a likeness once.

12

Demetrios very gently fanned
his skinny girl the other day
so not to cause discomfort and
he blew the girl away.

13

That earthquake made most everything
around start moving with its shock,
except this sprinter who stays crouching
still upon his starting block.

14

You ask my verdict on your two
portraits of Juno and of Jove;
flush the first one down the loo
and stuff the other in the stove.

METRODORUS* (4TH CENTURY AD)

1

John spent a quarter of his life
in boyhood, and a fifth in youth,
a third in manhood, then, grown old,
had thirteen years to wait for death.

2

Annette, harvesting the apples,
shared them out among the girls;
Janet got a fifth for portion,
Joan a fourth, while little Pearl
took a nineteenth, Jill a tenth;
a twentieth went to Rose-Marie,
but poor Diane got only twelve:
Annette herself decided she
had no necessity for more
than an adequate six score.

3

There are four taps to the tank.
The first can fill it in a day;
the second takes two days; the third
needs three, the fourth one four: now weigh
The matter up and say how long
the job would take with all taps on.

*The answers to these arithmetical problems are:
1. 15 in boyhood, 12 as youth, 20 as man,
   and 13 as old man, making 60 years altogether.
2. There were 380 apples.
3. Twelve twenty-fifths of a day.

NICARCHUS (1st century AD)

1

Does Henry sigh, or does he fart?
His breath's as strong from either part!

2

If blocked, a fart can kill a man;
if let escape, a fart can sing
health-giving songs; farts kill and save:
a fart is powerful as a king.

PHILEMON

Had I been certain that the dead
were sensate and had faculties
I would have hanged myself to get
a glimpse of great Euripides.

PALLADAS (FL. AD 400)

1

Zeus, you're a cold fish
not to alter
into a bull or swan
to mount this creature;

she's as delectable
from head to foot
as ever Danae
welcoming the wet,

or Leda splayed
submissive by her pool,
or even Europa
bold with her big bull.

But I expect
you're too stuck-up to act
on any whore,
however she attracts.

for, after all,
you've never made a pass
at any girl
not virgin, or high-class.

2

A woman is a maddening creature
and gives pleasure twice at most,
once when she gives up her virtue,
once when she gives up the ghost.

3

It's wisest for the ignorant chap
to hide his verbiage like a clap.

4

Naked I came,
and naked I return.
Why do I sweat
to fill the naked urn?

5

What good do you do anyone
by writing verses, getting cash
for silly slanders, peddling iambs
as a huckster peddles trash?

6

Shakespeare came to Larry's bed
as he lay sleeping still;
"I never did you harm" he said,
"Why do you speak me ill?"

7

Even ants and gnats have spleens.
If these creatures are allowed
their angers, why should I be asked
to patiently accept the loud
attacks of everyone, not ever
answer vicious deeds with seething
words, but gag myself and spend
my lifelong day not even breathing?

8

God detests the belly
for it must
be blamed for appetites
that lead to lust.

9

Them hats and boots and bits of spears
Sergeant Clodd gives Holy Zears.

10

Money, Money, flattery's father,
product both of pain and care,
it is frightening to possess you,
but agony when you aren't there!

11

Here, beside his statue, Block
is dumb and steady as a rock;
he seems so stony that I itch
to know which marble copies which.

12

Ponder how your father got you
and abandon vanity!
Plato may have swelled your ego,
babbling "Immortality,"

blathering of a "Heavenly Plant,"
but another voice would cry
"You are nothing but the dust";
yet this is still a pretty lie,

glossing over brutal facts
with rhetoric, for if you face
the truth, you're got by helpless lust
and wetness in a filthy place

13

From conjugating with a man
the Grammarians' daughter
bore a child that was, by turns
masculine, feminine, and neuter.

14

Monks are solitaries, yet
there are so many that I get
to wonder how so big a crowd
can make pretence of solitude.

15

Life is a theatre, a play:
either put your wisdom by
and learn the method to perform,
or bear your suffering patiently.

16

The man whose wife is filled with spite
turns up the lamp to gain some light
each evening and finds only night.

17

We are new-made every dawn;
the days before it have all gone;
our yesterdays have flown away;
what's left of life begins today.
Old men, don't bitch about past years,
they're lost and are no longer yours.

PHILLIPUS

1

Ancient Nico placed these flowers
upon Melites' maiden tomb.
Hades, did you use your powers
properly choosing which to doom?

PHILIPPUS OF THESSALONICA
(2ND CENTURY AD)

1

Fisher Jack, now bent with age,
his hands grown shaky, dedicates
to Hermes these: his rods, their lines
looped slackly, and his oars that late
swam lithe as fish, his shining hooks
that caught the fishes by the throat,
his lead-fringed nets, his paternoster,
and the gently bobbing floats
that told him where his tackle hung,
his pair of wicker creels, his warm
unfailing lamp, his anchor that
traps wandering boats and holds them firm.

2

I, a ship, built on the profits
from my master's amorous trade,
slide into the sea the Goddess
took as birthplace. He that made
my beauty calls me Courtesan,
for I am kind to one and all;
board me boldly; I don't ask
a lot for passage, and instal
most gladly those who wish to come —
natives, aliens, every fellow —
and I ride as well on land
as on the sweet tempestuous billow.

3

The miller owned me while he lived,
a hoarse reverberant millstone
that crushed the wheat, Demeter's slave,
and when he died they placed me on
his tomb as emblem of his trade
a thing perpetually heavy
all his days, and now he's dead
as weighty still upon his body.

RUFINUS (1ST OR 2ND CENTURY AD)

THE COMPLETE POEMS

1

She swears she's not in love. She lies.
Her every gesture shows love's pain:
her shallow breath, her smiles, her sighs,
and, under sleepless eyes, the stain.
Return, winged Loves, and plague her wits,
hurl yet more arrows from above
and torture her till she admits,
humiliated, "I'm in love."

2

I and she the other day
took out a bat and ball to play.
She giggled when I said "Dear chump,
that's the twelfth time I've hit your stump;
tomorrow morning I will score
the same, I'm sure, and maybe more."

The next day, when she came to play
I told her, laughing, "I must say
I can't think why I don't invite
you to a different game by night."

3

She was fifteen and lived next door; she sent
me crazy for her; she would smile and tease
and give a little cry each time I took
a chance and slid my hand above her knees.
But who respects a blush? She felt some pain,
but I was careful not to be too rough,
and we succeeded. Now she's two months gone,
so should I face the music or clear off?

4

Alone at last with lovely Lais,
I whispered as I stroked her knee
that there was nothing left in life
if she would not give in to me;
I was so eloquent she cried
and I felt eased of every doubt,
but when I murmured "Oh, my Bride!"
she dried her eyes and threw me out.

5

Many, many times I've longed
to have and hold you through the night,
my Thalia, and with urgent, strong
possession glut my appetite,
but now, though you lie naked here
and press against me in the bed,
I fail, collapse. It will not stir
or lift its fat and torpid head.
You wretched creature! Why so slack?
Stand up! Stand up! Be vigorous,
for soon enough you'll grieve to lack
such luck and such a happiness.

6

Europa's kiss is sweet when it caresses
lightly, lip and lip scarce meeting, but
when open-mouthed with leaping tongue she kisses
she drags your very soul out by the root.

7

My wish for you, though far away,
is happiness if this can be.
Myself, I weep the nights away,
my lone bed stained with misery.
Here on Coressus I complain
and in Artemis' shrine. But I
will meet your eyes tomorrow when
I'll tell you this. Till then, Goodbye.

8

How long, Prodike, must I
cower weeping at your door,
how long, you cruel creature, cry
these pleas and prayers that you ignore?
White threads already touch your hair
and all too quickly we will be
too old for all that we should share,
I Priam and you Hecube.

9

Cynthia prides herself upon
the beauty of her face and figure,
and when I meet her gives the frown
a Lady gives a loathsome beggar;
my gifts of flowers go in the bin;
my notes are burned; may age, unkind
with aches and wrinkles, quickly bring
vain Cynthia cause to change her mind.

10

Reason armours me with mail
to battle Love and one to one,
through man to god, I cannot fail,
but should flushed Bacchus come upon
the scene and give my foe his aid
it's two to one and I'm outplayed.

11

Let's bathe, my love, and have some sport;
let's crown ourselves with wreaths and drink
the good strong wine, lift glasses, clink,
the life of happiness is short,
and in old age these pleasures pall,
while death takes all.

Or, alternatively

Sweet Julia, let us bathe together,
lounge in gowns and sip champagne;
pleasure does not last for ever;
age too soon begins to maim
these limbs whose joys, entwined, we spend,
and death's the end.

12

Praxiteles is dead and gone,
and too, the skilful Polycleitus
who moulded living flesh from stone
and gave us breathing smiling statues.
Now there's no sculptor that expresses
Melissa's eyes of fire, her bare
and lucent throat, her fragrant tresses.
Where are the artists now, oh where?
Such beauty is so rare and fine
it cries for genius and a shrine.

13

Glorious Hera, golden shod,
and Athene lately saw
Maeonis and with passion said
"One judgement is enough. No more
will we strip naked for men's eyes
and lose another beauty prize.

14

My darling, it was Eros took
me to your household as a slave;
my ox-broad shoulders bore your yoke;
I ploughed love's furrow deep and gave
my eager body to love's chains,
and I will never plead to be
freed from my serfdom or to gain
the bitterness of liberty –
at least until old age has laid
its chill hand upon lip and thigh.
Oh, may our fortune long evade
the sorcery of Time's evil eye.

15

I love you absolutely, but
I can't admire your roving eyes,
especially when I see them light
on dreadful men that I despise.

16

Bathing, silver-footed in the stream,
her apple breasts as white as clotted cream,
her twin posteriors circling round to show
they flow more smoothly than the waters flow,
spread fingers proved inadequate to hide
the whole of her deep fountain – but she tried.

17

Gods, I swear I did not see
naked Cypris bathing there,
unloosening her hair to free
it to her shoulders glistening bare.
Have mercy, O great Goddess! Do
not blind my peeping eyes with wrath!
But now I see it isn't you
but Rhodoclea takes a bath.
How come so lovely? Can it be
that she has robbed divinity?

18

This crown of flowers, Rhodope,
I made myself for you.
Here's a blushing rose and here
a daffodil still pearled with dew,
a lily, an anaemone,
a violet from the shade.
Wear it, my dear, with modesty
for girls, like flowers, fade.

19

Those two hookers, "Gig" and "Dinghy,"
always drifting round the docks,
are extremely dangerous, sonny;
don't be misled by their looks!
Though they're trim and freshly painted,
pointed bow and bobbing stern
are traps for sailors; if you board them
you will either drown or burn!

20

Darling, you possess both Hera's
eyes and Aphrodite's breasts.
the feet of Thetis and Athene's
fingers; it's sheer happiness
just to look on you like this,
and when you speak to me to hear.
Your kiss is ultimate Paradise,
your bed immortal bliss, my dear.

21

Your lips are pure persuasion; you
have all the charms of Aphrodite,
the voice of Calliope too,
the Hours' freshness; dancing lightly,
your fingers are Athene's own,
your judgement Themis'. Therefore,
since you are all, and yet are one,
three Graces have been changed to four.

22

If, Love, you shoot arrows through
both hearts at once, then you're a true
and proper god and playing fair,
but if you don't, no god I swear.

23

Lamplighter Love, if you can't flame
desire in both of us the same,
please quench or take away this hot
fire that I feel but she does not.

24

Admit I warned you, Helen. "Soon enough
we'll age and love decay and fail," I said,
"a net of wrinkles pursing up your mouth,
and hair as grey as ash upon your head."

And so, my dear, who trembles for your kiss
and aches for more, or pleads to take you home
through clinging twilight, now your beauty is
as pocked and weathered as a graveyard stone?

25

Why aren't you, Belle, the girl you've always been —
stepped straight out of a glossy magazine
with swinging hips, bold make-up, bolder eyes,
and cool disdainful poise? Cut down to size,
your body's thickened now, your face gone coarse —
it is the usual fate for stuck-up whores!

Or, alternatively,

Melissa, where's your golden glory fled,
your gowns, your pearls, your mirror's admiration,
your wild capricious whims, your proud held head,
your trim slim ankles and your ostentation?
Now you're old, draggle-haired, with swollen feet;
well, that's the fate conceited whores must meet.

26

She who once upon a time
was smooth of skin and round of breast,
her carriage proud, her ankle slim,
eyebrows well shaped, hair deftly dressed,
old age has sadly redesigned;
her sometime beauty no-one sees —
only a wig and brows more lined
than any grinning chimpanzee's

27

Now age has sagged that flawless shape
and wrinkled skin once smooth as marble,
and thinned that hair that swept your nape
so sensually, you flirt, are playful.
It's much too late. Be off! Retire!
I sought the rose and not the briar.

28

When you take a woman, choose
to have one that is neither plump
nor slender; averages are best —
the first will wear you to a stump,
the second hurt you with her sharp
protruding bones. In love, I guess,
it's as in other matters: neither
starve nor suffer from excess!

29

I hate a girl that's easy meat;
prudes also I avoid and hate:
the one says "yes" before I've asked;
the others wait till it's too late.

30

I prefer slave girls to well bred women,
not being fond of high-priced luxuries.
With those it's perfume, vanities, and presents,
and perilous concealed adulteries,
but with these love's natural and pleasant,
no whims, caprices, or unreasoning strife.
I emulate sagacious Pyrrhus who
preferred dear Andromache to his wife.

31

They say I've turned from chasing boys
to being crazy for the girls,
from natural bloom and naked skin
to lipstick, powder, rouge, and curls.
Sure, there are dolphins in the trees,
and stags are grazing on the seas.

32
Who is responsible for this?
a girl thrown out into the street
without a stitch! Excuse me, Miss,
but he must be a fool to treat
a lovely girl like you that way!
Did he discover you in bed
with someone else? All women play
that trick at times. Don't hang your head.
It's quite the usual thing, my sweet;
so next time that he takes a trip
and you are tempted, don't retreat
and let the chance of pleasure slip,
but use your head as well: before
you start, make sure you've locked the door.

33
What brute would strip his wife and turn her out
into the street for going with a man,
pretending that at no time in his life
has he had whores, the lying puritan?
But also what absurd young wife would wail
and weep and spoil her looks with tears before
the madman's door? Stop sobbing. Without fail
we'll find another man for you, what's more
one that won't beat his wife the slightest bit
or grow curious where she's getting it.

34

Her eyes are filled with hazel light;
her skin is soft; her lips are moist
and crimson as a rose; her neck
is pearly as her heaving breasts,
those Goddess breasts! What if, among
her hair that's raven as the night
a little thistledown has blown?
I would not care if it were white.

35

Time has not withered you; in age
your shining apples, your moist rose,
retain that beauty that has burned
more hearts to ashes than it knows.

36

Melite, Rhodope and Rhodoclea
once on a time decided that they should
compete to find which pretty one of them
had the most lovely lure of womanhood,
They made me judge and posed before me as
if they were goddesses, divinely nude.
Rhodope was the first on whom I gazed
and what her spread thighs showed me was bedewed
and filled with honey as an opening rose
stirred by a breeze and gently quivering,
but Rhodoclea's shone like polished glass
shaped into smoothness, moistly glistening
as if it had been carved to grace a shrine—
then suddenly it all came back to me—
what Paris got for playing judge like this—
I promptly crowned the whole immortal three.

37

These three, wondering which of their
firm bottoms was the loveliest,
called me to judge, and, stripping bare,
put their posteriors to the test.
The first was petal-soft and white,
each buttock beauty, pure and simple,
on each round cheek, neat, delicate
and magical, a little dimple
The second, spreading snowy thighs,
revealed a many-petalled rose
that blushed more rose to meet my eyes,
while on the third to take the pose
a ripple stirred voluptuous skin
as if by some warm dream inspired.
Had Paris, who was once required
to judge three Goddesses, been in
my place he would not, I maintain,
think on those Goddesses again.

38

If only feminine attractions
could survive concluded actions,
no man ever would require
varying prospects to desire!

Unhappily, it is the law
that, once they've bedded, women bore.

SATYRUS

Echo, tongueless, sings her sweet
and mimic song in sheep-strewn meadows,
taking up the words of birds
and making her own songs their shadows.

STRATO (2ND OR 3RD CENTURY AD)

1

Though in the street I take good care
never to openly admire
an approaching boy, or stare
into his face, the old desire
grips me still; once he's gone by
I turn and glut my hungry eye.

2

As you lean, you press that splendid bottom
warmly against the cold chill of the wall;
My Darling Boy, why offer that temptation
to mere stone that can't respond at all?

3

When a boy gains my affection
and I kiss him, I detest
angry words of protestation,
struggling hands and thumping fists,

but a boy that, once within my
arms, is eager for his fate
and straightway ready to abandon
every shame, I also hate,

preferring one that knows the way to
give himself and not to give,
restrained yet passionate, neither shamed
nor too inflamed by acts of love.

4

My Darling Boy, if you feel it was wrong
of me to kiss you, if I've caused you pain,
then punish me as I deserve; inflict
the same abuse, and kiss me back again.

5

I swore I'd never breathe a single
syllable of what he said,
not even tell it to myself,
but hidden joy's as good as dead,
and I must shout it out aloud,
no matter what. *He said I could!*
What point is there in having luck
if no-one knows it's any good?

6

Sex and booze don't last for ever;
once we're boxed the fun is through;
so, each day till we're dug under,
Darling, let us drink and screw.
Let's live it up until there's doubt
if even Hell can dry us out!

7

Julian, when I said Goodnight,
kissed me – or was it a dream?
The rest is clear enough, alright, –
our talk, his question, where we'd been –
but, did he kiss me? Was it real?
I can't be certain. If he did,
why am I walking in the street
who, surely, have become a god?

8

Those pretty boys in pretty clothes,
My Dear, won't heed our smiles or words;
the highest peaches on the tree,
they're strictly for the wasps and birds!

9

My neighbour's tender little boy
teases with flirtatious laughter,
hinting willingness; though young,
it's clear he knows what I am after,
and the green fruit swells unguarded;
but, when ripe and fit for plucking,
there'll be barbed wire, dogs, and fences,
and a jealous gardener looking!

10

As Adrian's naked bottom pressed
that wooden bench, it pinched his cheeks;
I tremble to love such a boy
that even wood desires and tweaks.

11

Though on his cheeks fine down is curling,
and other, crisper hairs have reared,
I swear I'll never leave my darling,
however marred by hairs or beard.

12

I may be hooked, but I'm not caught
completely, dear. You have to play
me cunningly; keep that line taut
or I will surely get away.

13

Were you still innocent, I wouldn't mind;
I'd sympathise, for you might well suppose
the business formidable, be afraid:
but really, Darling, since the whole world knows

your rich friend's taught you everything, and paid
you well for it, and that you are proficient,
even adept, why refuse me what
he takes indifferently? There is sufficient

reason, surely! Pushed out of his bed
once you've been used, so he can get to sleep,
you're played with and not loved. Come home with me
and what a different company you'll keep!

We'll game together, walk together, talk
as equals, and what else we do we'll do
from mutual wishes; no more love to order!
Though, of course, I'll pay you for it, too!

14

You laugh, laugh, laugh, and never say
a single word. How do I stand it?
I plead. You laugh. I plead again,
and get no answer. I demand it,
beg it, weep . . . You cruel lout,
there's nothing here to laugh about!

15

Say Yes, say Yes, and take my cash!
Already wealthy? Then you are
benign enough, I hope, to press
your favours on the naked poor. . . .

THE EMPEROR TRAJAN

With gaping mouth and monstrous nose
should your dial face the moving sun,
finally you'll be of use
to tell the time to everyone.

Or, alternatively,

Point your nose up to the sky,
Your mouth agape, and passers by
will pause beside you, stare, and say
how well you tell the time of day.

VI

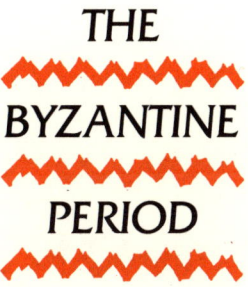
THE
BYZANTINE
PERIOD

AD 500 – AD 1000

AGATHIAS (AD 536–582)

In this privy well-sauced duck
has lost its charm and turned to muck.
Partridge, pheasant, caviare, hams
larks' tongues, pâtés, crabs and clams,
oysters, olives, vine leaves, veal,
become a dung-heap, every meal
first in then out. Just think of it!
We paid good money for this shit.

DAMASKIOS (FL. AD 529)

Her body, not her spirit, was enslaved;
now that, too, has the freedom that she craved.

ERATOSTHENES SCHOLASTICUS
(6TH CENTURY AD)

1

Herewith drunken William gives
you, Bacchus, this great empty vat.
Thank him warmly, for it is
the only fortune he has got.

2

How glorious is virginity!
And yet we may be sure
if all of us chose chastity
the race would not endure.

Marriage is a better plan.
Marry with acuity
and give birth to another man,
ensuring perpetuity.

Shun promiscuity.

JULIAN ANTECESSOR (6TH CENTURY AD)

His beard's so thick
I think that Dick'll
give up scissors
for a sickle.

JULIANUS, PREFECT OF EGYPT
(6TH CENTURY AD)

1

Elizabeth delights to make
her men friends crazy with desires
she never satisfies. Just Gods,
give her the fate the case requires –

not death, but dotage – falling hair,
hard wrinkles – for her beauty's made
so many sinful thoughts it's sinned
itself, and ought to be betrayed.

2

I often said, and still I say
"Drink up! Like me, you'll soon be clay."

3

You gave me beauty, Cytherea,
but gradual time has withered me;
now, since your gift is gone, I give
the glass that kept it company.

4

John gives the nymphs this net, for age
no longer has the strength to free
its folds and cast. Feed easy, fish.
Age gives your seas their liberty.

5

"You died of booze, Anacreon!"
I admit that's true,
but you who've stayed upon the wagon
will land in Hades too!

6

He painted her exactly how she was;
no artist could have shown her glory better,
yet now we wish that he had failed because
our grief's so sharp we're desperate to forget her.

7

Among the flowers that I wove
to make a wreath, I found
secreted in the roses, Love.
I seized him and I drowned
him in my wine, drank hastily,
and now his wings are tickling me.

MACEDONIUS THE CONSUL (6TH CENTURY AD)

1

I've got dyspepsia from love;
I ache; I've wind around my heart:
why should it trouble me like this?
Can't it excite a different part?

2

"See you tomorrow, then." Tomorrow,
it is certain, never comes.
Evasions and delays recur.
The host of layabouts and bums
you run around with get your smiles,
your little gifts, your drinks. But I,
who love you, get a cool "Hello,"
a broken promise, and a lie.
"See you this evening, then!" But what
does "evening" mean to you? I'd gauge
it means not this, not next year, but
a wrinkled toothless haggard age.

3

At anchor in the holy temple of Neptune
Cretas' ship once sailed the turbulent ocean;
she rides before the wind no more, and he's
safe also now on shore and sleeps at ease.

PAUL THE SILENTIARY (FL. AD 560)

1

While I am kissing Anthony
I can't help thinking of John;
as John enjoys my nakedness
my mind is embracing Tom,
while Tom reminds me of William –
and that's how it goes on!

And why should I feel any shame
in following Venus's example?
Let her condemn who is frigid, plain,
or finds her husband really ample.

2

Under her Mother's nose
and avoiding her eye,
she slipped me a pair
of apples; as she pressed
them in my hands, Love rose
and made me curse
two apples in my grip
and not two breasts.

3

I had the gorgeous Jacqueline
for comapny all last night;
she never stopped complaining,
and even before the light
had faded she was blaming
the stars for bringing morning.

Nothing on earth is perfect;
something is always wrong:
girls like that need the North Pole
and a night six months long.

4

The fever's done. The fire is out.
I do not burn, but die of cold.
Love's finished me; its greedy heat
has eaten up my blood, and rolled
its lava through my bowels, veins,
and even bones. Now it is done.
The bonfire's out, and nothing's left
but drifting ash upon cold stone.

5

Your eyes look bruised and heavy, Dear,
as if still blurred with sleep; your hair
hangs lank and casual; your cheek
is damp and pale, you have an air
of sheer exhaustion. Why is this?
If it's because you've spent all night
in making love, I'd say the man
must surely have explored delight
into delirium; but if
it is frustrated love that's let
you get this way, then don't despair:
I'm willing, and not hard to get.

6

I'd rather have your wrinkles, Jane,
than any young girl's peach-bloom cheek,
and rather hold those nodding withered
apples in my hands than take
my pleasure of still ripening breasts
however plump, however firm;
such Springtimes may be delicate
but Autumn fires more fiercely burn,
and, O, your Winter's warmer far
than others' wanton summers are!

7

Zeus breached young Danae and her tower
as a golden rain,
and crudely cut her virgin knot.
The moral's pretty plain!

It's money conquers all the time;
it breaks through every wall,
snaps every handcuff, opens every
lock, and, above all,

makes womenfolk submit. Hard cash
brought Danae to her end.
No need to pray, or sigh, or plead
if you've enough to spend.

8

One afternoon I found Annette,
that pretty little thing, in bed,
and fast asleep, her naked arms
thrown, like a child's, above her head.
I seized my chance, and boldly slid
beside her, and, to my surprise,
was more than halfway there before
she woke, and with astounded cries
began to pull my hair and thump
with tiny fists my back and head;
she struggled until all was done,
then tearfully lay still and said:

"You brute. You've got your way at last,
although I swore I never should
and wouldn't touch your money. Now
you've had it you will leave for good
and never think of me again,
but find another girl to chase;
by hook or crook you'll share her bed
and have your will, then off you'll race
to someone else and start afresh
without a single twinge of shame,
insatiable! Don't say you won't.
I swear you men are all the same!"

9

Joyce's kiss is long and loud,
and Janice's is secret, warm,
while Janey's delicately bites:
judicially I weigh their form
and plan my vote – but where's the point?
Ann's kiss, that honeyed memory, lies
upon my lips. It's useless, girls!
Forget your bribes. Ann gets the prize.

10

I'm told that if a mad dog bites
a man, he sees the dog look up
at him from every pool. I see
your face in every brimming cup,
and sea, and river, oh my dear,
in every stream your face alone!
Do you suppose that Love ran mad
before it bit me to the bone?

11

"Goodbye" I almost say, but stop
convulsively, and linger still.
I cannot leave you. Parting shakes
my body like the fear of Hell.
Beside you, all is sweetness, light;
without you all the world is night.

12

Let's undress, Darling, and lie nude,
each knotted in the other's arms;
let nothing come between us: that
last nylon wisp which veils your charms
to me seems more a wall of stone!
Away with it! Unveil! Unbind!
Come close and kiss! I'll say no more.
I hate loose talk of any kind.

13

Why do you sneer at my grey hairs
and bloodshot eyes? You caused these sights –
the scars of unfulfilled desires,
the signatures of sleepless nights!
Yes, and the skin upon my ribs
is wrinkled as it is upon
my scrawny neck. The more I love
the more decrepit I become!
Take pity! Merely whisper "Yes,"
and straightaway my skin will get
its bloom again, my eyes grow bright,
my thick hair cluster black as jet.

14

For whom should I now comb and part my hair?
For whose soft cheek use after-shave? Why wear
this custom-tailored suit, this shot-silk tie?
My girl has gone and left me high and dry –
gone, gone, gone, and dully I must stare
on golden shining dawns bereft of her.

PLATO THE YOUNGER (1ST OR 2ND CENTURY AD)

I, the drunkard Dionysus,
am carved upon this amethyst.
Either this engraved device is
going to teach me to desist
or in due time it will have learned
itself to get completely stoned.

CONSTANTINE CEPHALAS (FL. AD 917)

As I warm to my task of teaching youth
with learned fervour, eagerly I touch
first upon love, for it is love that first
excites a boy to lifting the burning torch.

VII

ANONYMOUS

ANONYMOUS

1

I fell in love. I kissed, and she
required no compelling.
But who am I? And who is she?
I tell you, I'm not telling!

2

When your melons began to grow round
you let nobody touch them;
when they were big and ripe
you ignored my desire;
but now they are losing their shape
and starting to wither,
you'd put them in anyone's hands
that cares to enquire.

3

If you have ever glimpsed a boy
whose tender bloom stands out among
his playmates, radiant and supreme,
then you've discovered Johnathan.

And if at that first startling glance
you were not stricken to the bone
and flushed with feverish passion, you
must either be a god, or stone.

4

Grab every chance; all things decline.
You see a handsome kid. You dote.
And yet one summer is enough
to change him to a shaggy goat!

5

Hold your noise, you silly birds!
Why do you chatter so, as I
curl warmly here beside my boy?
Be quiet, nightingales, and try
a little sleep among those boughs.
You giggling women, hold your noise!

6

Whether I find you blonde or black,
brunette or redhead, every day
your young head troubles me with love,
as it will still when you are grey.

7

I wish I were a nodding rose
for you to watch me bud and blow,
and pluck me with that slender hand,
and press me to your breasts of snow.

8

Estella, that expensive whore
that has the whole town by the tail,
whose every breath means dollar bills
to those who venture to the sale,
slept with me naked in my dreams
the other night until the dawn,
and gave herself to me for free!
Now I don't have to stand her scorn
or face frustration. She comes cheap.
I only need to fall asleep!

9

Dionysus, once again
you stagger from the sacred flame
in glistening bronze to bless our earth,
for Myro's wrought your second birth.

10

Do not ridicule the small.
Little things can charm us all.
Eros was not big at all.

11

Traveller, if you pass by
Anacreon's grave I hope you'll stop
and pour a little wine, for all
my life I liked to take a drop.

12

A mere three dozen years of time
was all I got, but why protest?
At least I ended in my prime
and even Nestor died at last.

13

When Cypris once in Cnidus viewed
the Cypris there she blushed and hid
her face and cried "Whenever did
Praxiteles surprise me nude?"

14

Diogenes, among the shades,
his wise old age completed, saw
Croesus, laughed aloud, then spread
his tattered cloak upon the floor
beside the king who'd grabbed so much
good river gold, and said "I win!
For I've brought with me all I had,
and, Croesus, you lack everything!"

15

The dead are vomited by Hell;
the flesh of Christ has purged it well.

16

Son of God and Light of Light,
take this jade and corallite;
Son of God and of a Maid,
gifts of corallite and jade.

17

This cattle shed is Heaven now,
or greater far than Heaven, for
the whole of Heaven was the work
of this child huddled in the straw.

18

For angels and for men one song,
for God and Man are now as one.

19

Weep not for the happy dead
but those who think of death with dread.

20

There's no husband storms don't harry
men maintain, and then they marry.

21

Love, who protects the shipwrecked, grasp my hand;
I've come to grief and drown upon the land.

22

If only I were grown your glass
to gaze into your amorous eyes,
or changed into a silken dress
to slide upon your breasts and thighs,
or your perfume to warmly rest
on secret skin and sleep in hair,
or brassiere to cup your breasts,
or, worshipping the ground you tread,
if I were grown your high heel shoes,
bruised at each step I would be glad
of suffering such sweet abuse.

23

At his lectures seven's the amount
of students that Professor Deadwright meets,
no more, no less – that is if you should count
four blankly staring walls, three empty seats.

24

The dark earth and the trees both drink;
the falling rain's libations;
seas gulp down brooks and rivers and
the sun consumes the oceans;
the moon drinks up, it's said, the sun –
why can't I have a little one?

25

Here, ferry! Charon, over here!
The dog Diogenes demands attention.
He saw and spoke out coarse and clear
that life is nothing but pretension.

26

Borrow all you wish
and think of bankers
counting, counting, counting
with cramped fingers.

27

Do not ask whose grave this is,
but, Sailor, pray for easier seas.

28

Pleasures of the grape and grope
grease the steep descending slope.

29

Sixty and dead,
I never wed,
and wish my father
hadn't either.

30

Traveller, although this tomb
is very small, pour out some wine
upon the earth for you have come
upon a resting place divine
as any given deities;
here's Homer whom the Muses blessed
and honoured for his histories.
Traveller, do not hurry past.

31

Said Zeus to Love "I'm going to take
away your darts and thunder on."
Said Love "That would be a mistake!
You'll turn into a swan."